BULLDOZERS,
LOADERS,
AND SPREADERS

BULLDOZERS,
LOADERS,
AND SPREADERS

A Book About Roadbuilding Machines

THE 1973 NINTH GRADE ENGLISH CLASS
OF THE GREEN VALE SCHOOL, NANCY ARNAOUT, TEACHER

Mary Anderson	Sarah Fletcher
Victoria Butt	Alison Husting
Amy Clarkson	Marion Mundy
Alexandra Clifton	Devon Powers
Lillian Cushny	Nancy Toher
Lillian Doubleday	Cappy Von Stade

DOUBLEDAY & COMPANY, INC., GARDEN CITY, NEW YORK, 1974

ISBN 0-385-02375-8 Trade
        0-385-02376-6 Prebound
Library of Congress Catalog Card Number 73-10799
Copyright © 1974 by Doubleday & Company, Inc.
All Rights Reserved
Printed in the United States of America
9   8   7   6   5   4   3

PREFACE

This book was conceived as a project in a ninth-grade English class at Green Vale School, Glen Head, Long Island, New York. One teacher and twelve students worked together for several months planning, doing research, organizing and sorting out tremendous quantities of material as our requests began to bear fruit. The text was written by all thirteen of us, sometimes individually, sometimes in small groups, sometimes as a class. It would be difficult to imagine a group of twelve students who could work together as persistently and effectively as this class did. We have all, I think, gained as much from this experience of overcoming obstacles together as we have from seeing our efforts produce tangible results in the form of this book.

N.A.

BULLDOZERS,
LOADERS,
AND SPREADERS

There are many jobs that men cannot do without the help of heavy machines. One of the most important things that machines are used for is making roads. Have you ever thought how much work goes into building a road?

The land must be cleared before a road is built. Sometimes there are trees that have to be pushed down. In the fields and forests, powerful bulldozers clear the trees away.

Sometimes the bulldozer plows through deep, thick mud to get to the uncleared forest.

Logs weighing many tons are dragged out of the forest.

There are different machines for different jobs. The wheel loader has metal clamps that pick up the heaviest logs. With this machine, many logs can be lifted at the same time.

Sometimes there are big rocks that are in the way and have to be removed. If a rock is too big for a machine to move, dynamite is used to blast the rock away.

The land must be flat where a road is to be built. There is always extra dirt.
Bulldozers with their big blades must push the dirt away into piles.

The shovel on the backhoe loader picks up the dirt which the bulldozer has left and places it where it can be used again.

Roads must have pipes to drain off rainwater and melting snow. Roads become slippery if the water is not removed. The pipes are put underground so that they are not a hazard. Ditches must be dug to lay the pipes beneath the soil.

When the pipe is very big, the ditches must be deep. The long arm on the backhoe loader can dig these deep ditches or trenches.

The long heavy pipes are carried to the ditches after they are dug. The huge pipes are too heavy for men to carry. The wheel loader, another big machine, has clamps like big hands that hold the pipes and carry them to the trenches.

Pipes come in all different lengths. There are long pipes, thin pipes, short ones, and fat ones. The pipes are laid beside the ditch.

Sturdy chains are used to lower the pipes into the trenches. The machine can lay the pipe exactly in the middle of the ditch.

When the pipes are finally in the ditch, they are joined together. Several men work to do this.

After the pipes are connected, they look like a long sleeping snake. The men use machines to cover the pipes with dirt. Now nobody traveling on the road can see the big pipes. It is safer to drive because the water is drained off the road. Now the road is ready to be paved.

Before a road can be paved, a machine called a scraper scrapes the topsoil off the cleared land.

A motor grader has a strong, sharp blade under it. This long blade pushes the leftover dirt into many huge piles.

A loader's large shovel scoops up the soil that the motor grader has left behind. Heavy machines and dump trucks are used to help workmen take the tons of dirt away.

Some scrapers have a water tank in place of the blade. The machine carries the water tank in the back instead of carrying the blade underneath. The water is sprayed from the tank in many directions to wet the dirt road. This is done to keep the loose dirt from blowing away.

A loader scoops up the gravel and stones and dumps them into a truck. This truck takes the gravel to the unfinished road.

A machine spreads gravel on the smoothed dirt. The gravel is flattened by a heavy roller or leveled by a big rake. Some driveways and country roads are finished at this stage.

For most roads and highways, a huge concrete mixer pours wet bumpy concrete onto the gravel.

After the concrete has been poured, several different machines work together to finish the road.

One machine, called a slipform paver, is used to spread the concrete evenly over the surface of the road.

The same machine that spreads the concrete levels the surface and shapes the edges of the road.

A roller underneath the paving machine makes the damp concrete absolutely smooth and finishes the surface of the road. When the concrete has dried, lines are painted on the road to separate one lane from another. Now trucks, buses, and cars will be able to travel on the new road.

625.7 Green Vale School.
GRE c.2 Ninth Grade English
        Class, 1973

    Bulldozers, loaders,
      and spreaders

DATE			
5 MAR 1981 210			
MY 19 '81 153			
SEP 18 '81 235			
No 10 '81 203			
Do 8 '81 210			
Ja 11 '82 203			
Fe 09 '82 203			
NOV 28 1984 233			

No Record